A Kalmus Classic Edition

Henry
SCHRADIECK

SCHOOL OF VIOLA TECHNIQUE

VOLUME I

FOR VIOLA

K 04289

School of Viola Technique

First Division
Exercises on one string
1.
Repeat each number four times.

Transcribed by LOUIS PAGELS

1.

HENRY SCHRADIECK

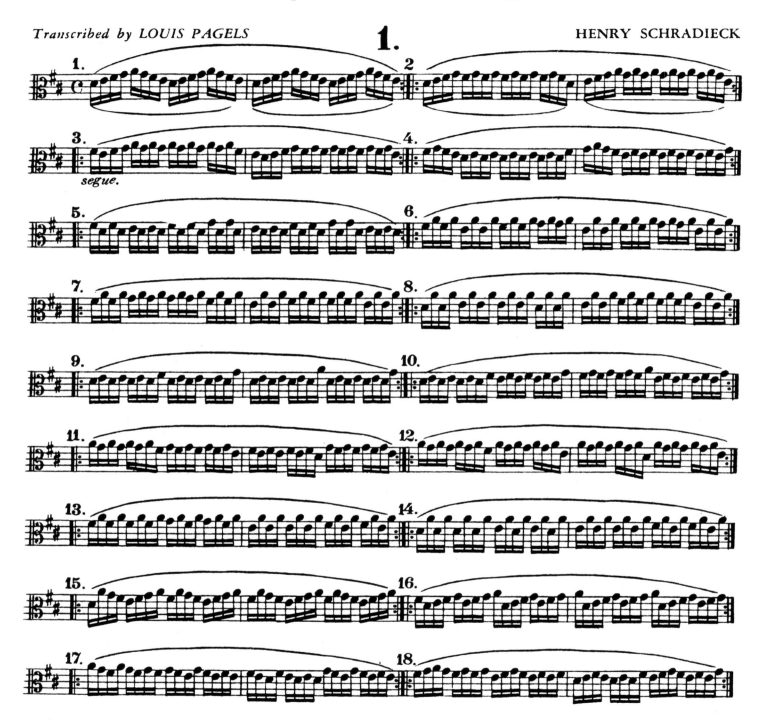

The pupil should attend to keeping the hand perfectly quiet in all the exercises, letting the fingers fall down strongly and raising them with elasticity. The movement according to the ability of the pupil must be lessened or accelerated, but is generally moderate.

EDWIN F. KALMUS
PUBLISHER OF MUSIC

4

3.

Exercises on two strings

4.

Exercises to be practiced by the wrist by keeping the right arm perfectly quiet.

5.

Exercises on 3 strings

6.

Exercises on 4 strings

7.

8.

Exercises in the second position

9.

Exercises in the first and second position

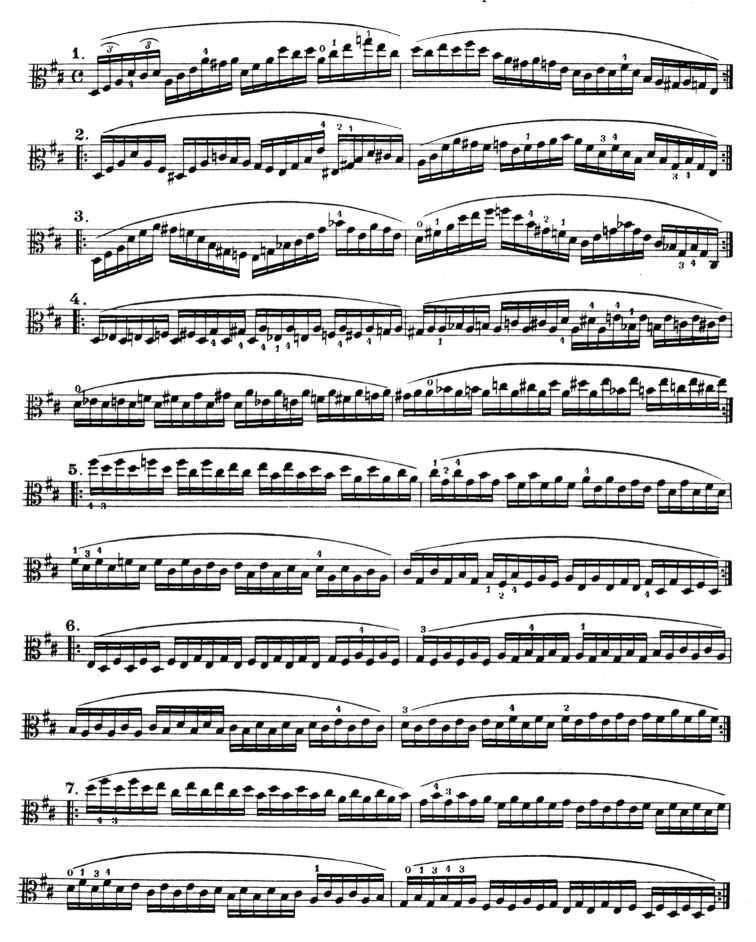

10.

Exercises in the third position

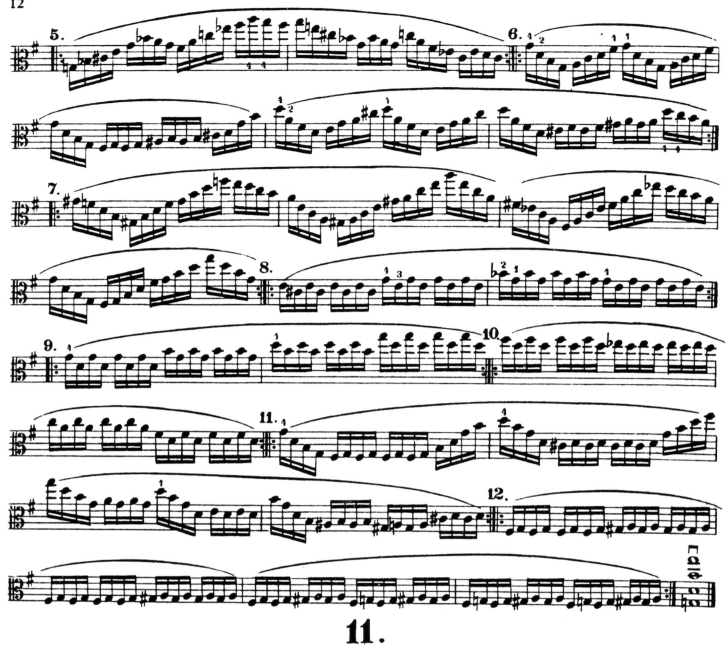

11.

Exercises in the first, second and third position

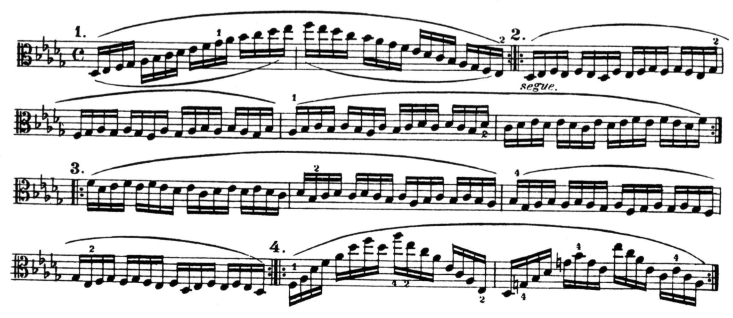

12.
Exercises on the fourth position

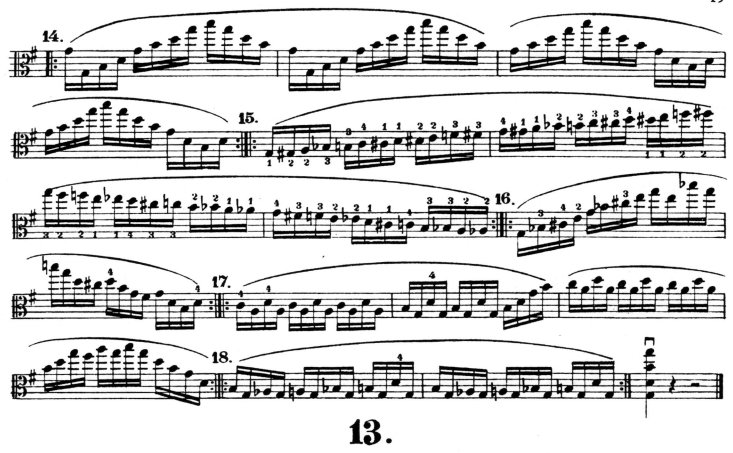

13.

Exercises in the first, second, third and fourth position

16

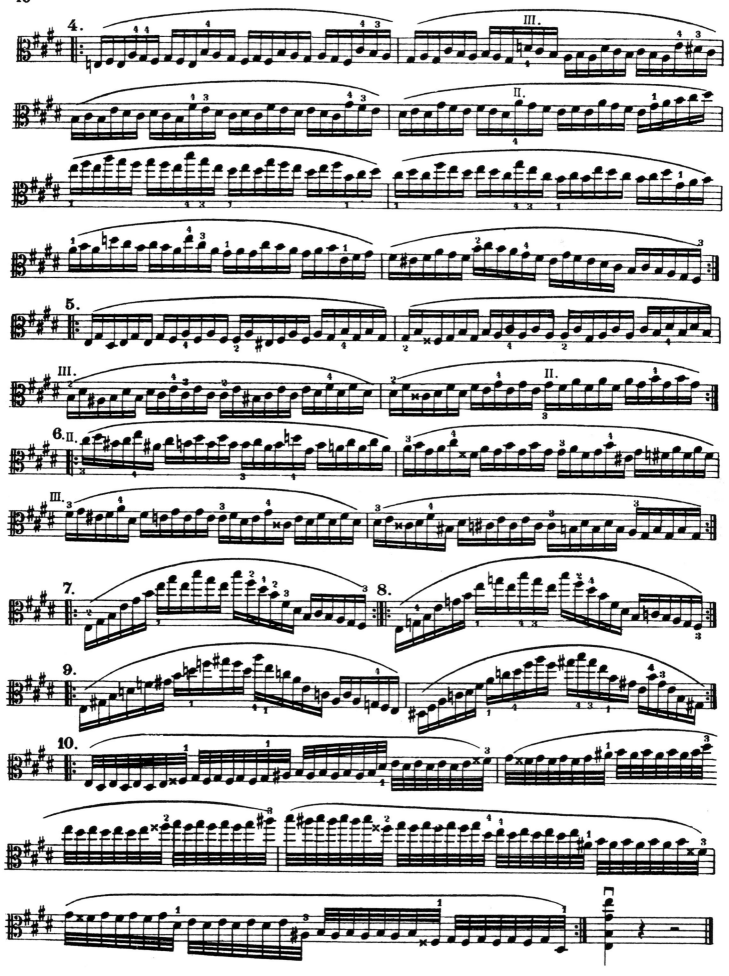

14.

Exercises in the fifth position

15.

Exercises passing through five positions

16.

Exercises in the sixth position

20

17.

Exercises passing through six positions

22

18.

Exercises in the seventh position

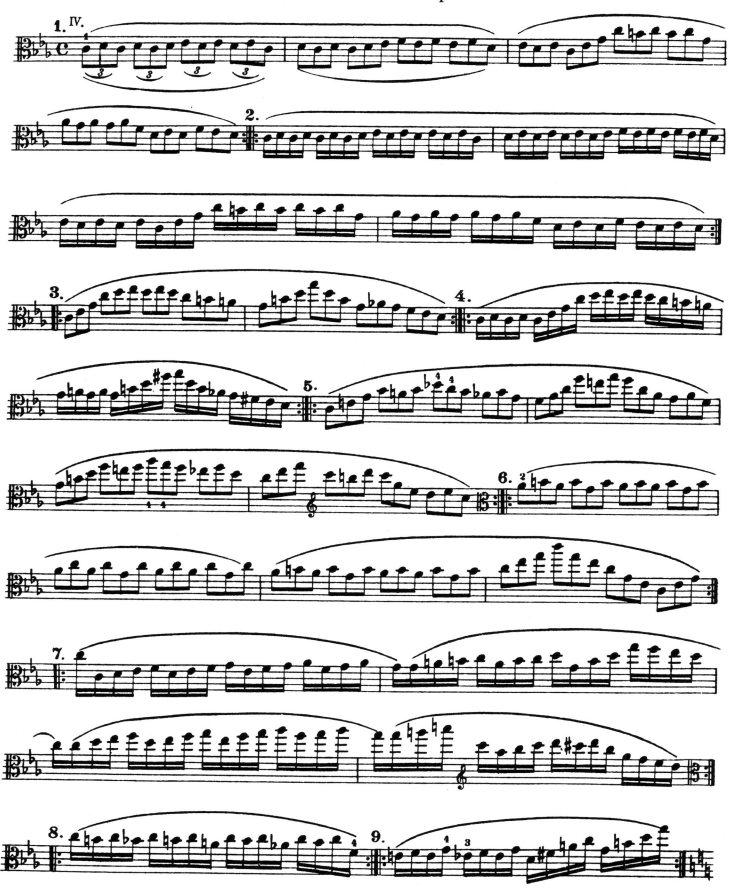

19.

Exercises passing through all positions

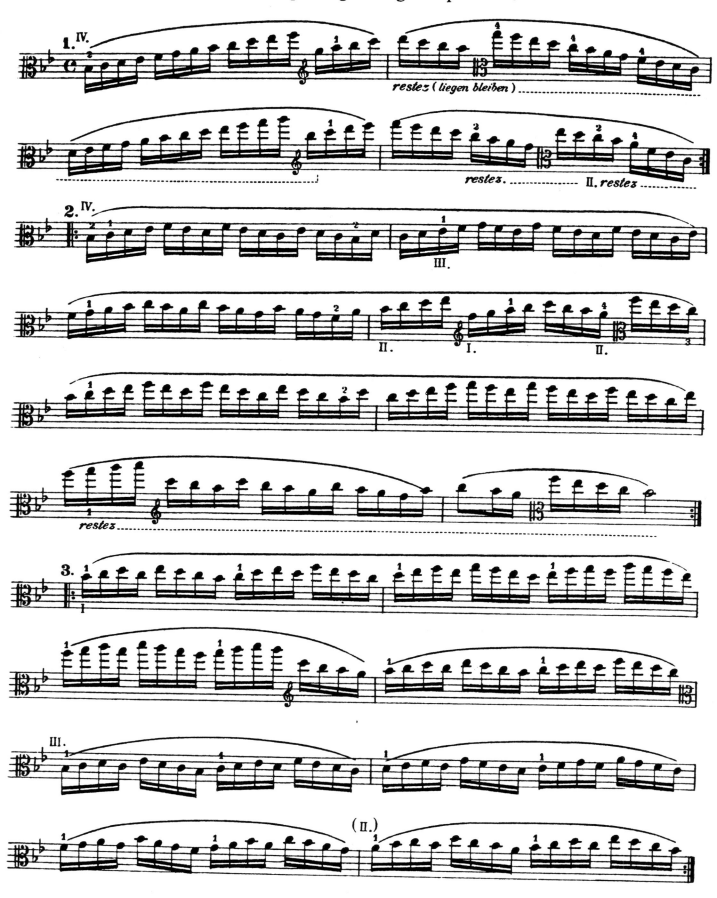

25

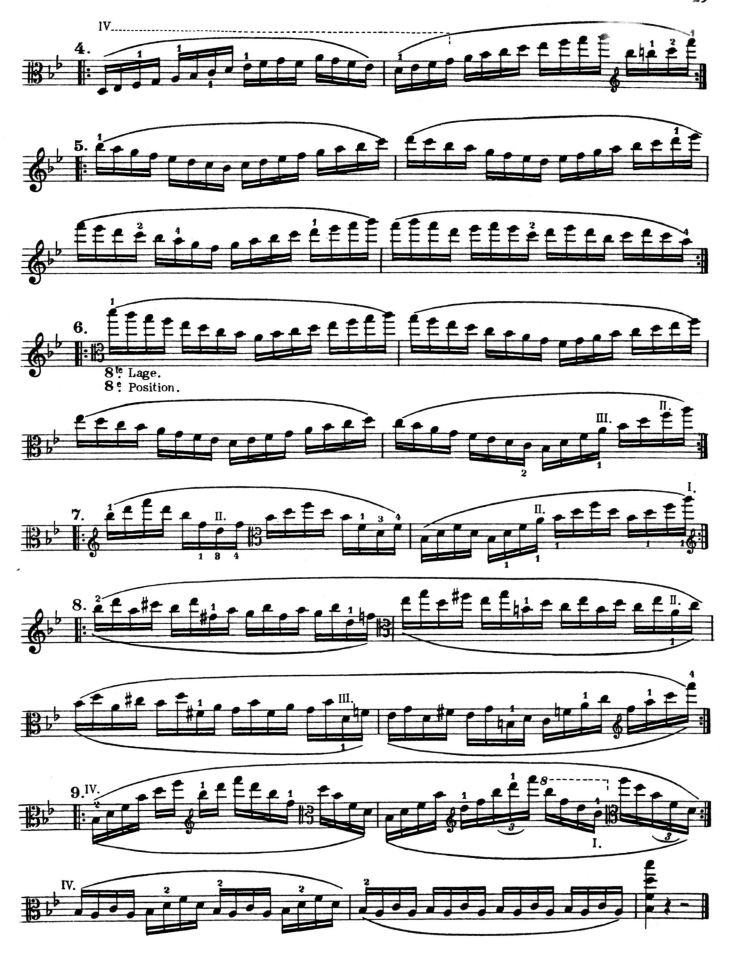

20.

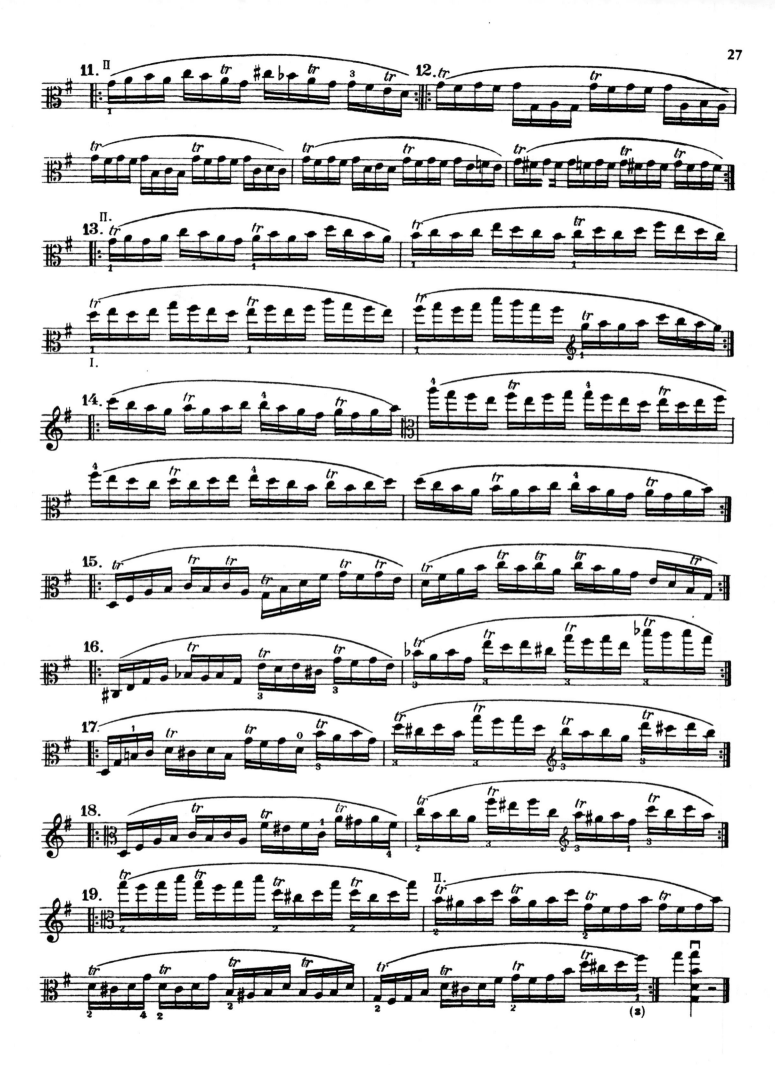